745.5 A566
35240032902232
31a
Andrews, Gavin (Gavin L.)
500 kids art ideas : inspiring projects for

WITHDRAWN

W9-BSD-888

500
Kids Art Ideas

500
Kids Art Ideas

Inspiring Projects for Fostering
Creativity and Self-Expression

Gavin Andrews

Quarry Books
100 Cummings Center, Suite 406L
Beverly, MA 01915

quarrybooks.com • www.craftside.net

CONTENTS

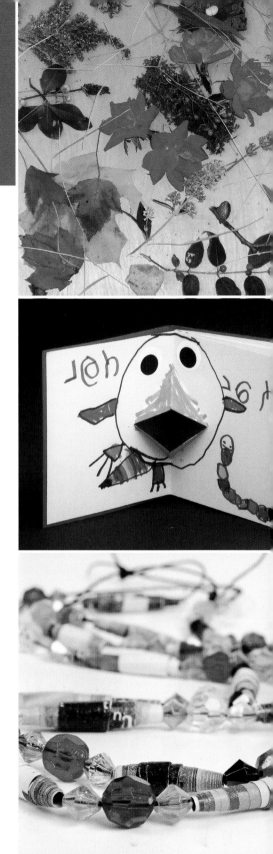

"Creativity is intelligence having fun."
—ALBERT EINSTEIN

About a year ago my oldest child was at home drawing and I asked him what he was making. He replied, "Something I have never seen before." I was blown away by this statement—and not just because he's my son! Did my three-year old really just say that? His reply illustrates how open and fearless young children are to creative experiences and new ideas. Anyone so willing to explore their creativity and imagination is truly an artist. The wonderful thing is, most kids are artists at heart!

This book is designed to explore the youngest artists in our lives and celebrate their natural and innate creativity. The projects range from simple to complex but all provide some inspiration to do something like it at home or school. Many of the kids featured likely had help from adults setting up their projects, but ultimately the artistic expression is their own. As parents and caregivers it's our job to provide the time, space and materials for these opportunities so that their minds can grow. Or as Einstein states - so their intelligence can have fun, which is in essence what learning is all about.

Various types of creative self-expression include imaginative play, exploring and reading books, listening and dancing to music, as well as art making. Each of these activities contributes to a child's growing capacity for learning. Creating art though is truly empowering for kids. As they create from their own imagination, there is something physical to see and reflect on once they are done. Asking kids to talk about what they create is a great way to build communication skills, inspire self-confidence and foster discussion about themselves and the world around them.

Making art can be as simple as handing your children a crayon and paper and letting them explore. The more they practice the more they can articulate, through art, their imagination and utilize their creative minds. Get creative alongside your child. Pick up a crayon, create a collage with torn paper or sculpt with aluminum foil and just be free. Create something that you have never seen before.

—Gavin Andrews

1. Felts, Fibers, and More

Felts, fibers, and other textiles are a rich well of materials that can be used to create exciting works of art that are not just for functional or useful purposes, such as bags or clothing. Imagine "drawing" images or words using yarn soaked in glue or weaving fibers to create beautiful abstract images. In this chapter, discover inventive uses of textiles, including decorated hand puppets and stuffed creatures made from scratch!

2. Made with Nature

The natural world is a wonderful source of not only creative inspiration, but also creative materials. Consider using leaves, twigs, and even rocks as painter's tools. Whether it's exploring natural materials to create temporary, ephemeral creative expressions in the forest or at the beach, or using found objects collected on nature walks to make collages, nature is an artist's playground.

016   Nature Walk Collage, Zack Peebles, Age 8;
Materials: Dried flowers, seeds, thistles, leaves,
bark, twigs and berries and roses

017   Nature Collage, For ArtSake Artists, Age 11, from Roxanne Evans Stout's River Garden Studio.
Materials: found objects from nature

018   Sand Art, Gage Minard, Age 10;
Materials: beach sand

019   Beach Wave, Kyle Browne's art students, Jamaica Plain, MA ages 5 and up; Materials: found beach objects

020　Nature Collage, For ArtSake Artists Age 11 from Roxanne Evans Stout's River Garden Studio; Materials: found objects from nature

021　Flower Mandala, Art in the Park with Kyle Browne, Jamaica Plain, MA, Ages 5–11; Materials: mandala inspired by the materials, shapes and patterns found in the natural world.

022　Twigs, Sunshine Academy Preschool Program, Brookline, MA; Materials: Found twigs, glue and cardstock

023　Nature Walk Collage, Nick Peebles, Age 8; Materials: Dried flowers, seeds, thistles, leaves, bark, twigs and berries and roses

024 Nature Collage, Susan Schwake's Art Lab students; Materials: Tree bark, small leaves, branches and paper glued on wooden panel

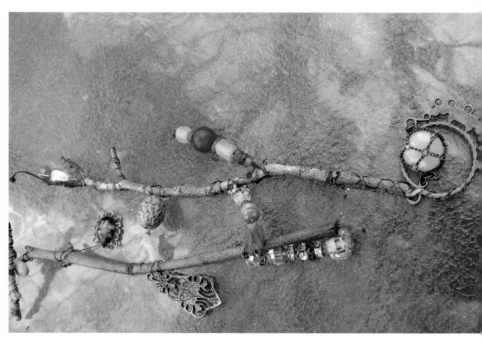

025 Ladder of Hope, For ArtSake Artists, Age 9–12 from Roxanne Evans Stout's River Garden Studio; Materials: sticks, wire, beads and found objects

026 Leaf Collage, Sunshine Academy Preschool Program, Brookline, MA; Materials: found leaves and contact paper

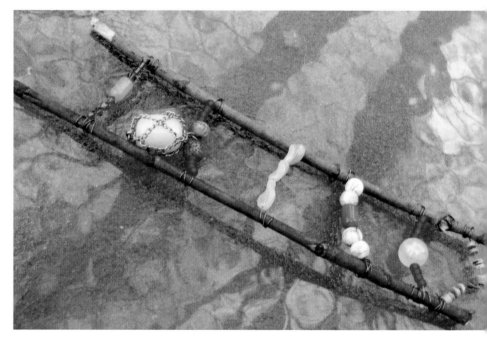

027 Nature Collage, For ArtSake Artists Age 11 from Roxanne Evans Stout's River Garden Studio; Materials: found objects from nature

028 Nature Mandala, Art in the Park with Kyle Browne, Jamaica Plain, MA, Ages 5–11; Materials: mandala inspired by the materials, shapes and patterns found in the natural world.

029 Fish Mandala, Art in the Park with Kyle Browne, Jamaica Plain, MA, Ages 5–11; Materials: mandala inspired by the materials, shapes and patterns found in the natural world.

030 Love You, Gavin Minard, Age 10; Materials: natural materials, flowers, sticks, and leaves

031 Nature Collage, Gavin Minard, Age 10; Materials: natural materials, flowers, sticks, and leaves

032   Falling Leaves, Sunshine Academy Toddler Program, Brookline, MA; Materials: found leaves, butcher paper and paint

033   Seed Filled Cascarones, Sebastian and Poppy Stubson, Ages 5 and 2½; Materials: egg shells, watercolor paints, perennial seeds, tissue paper and glue.

034   Beach Mural, Sunshine Academy Infant Program, Brookline, MA; Materials: Sand, paint, glue and paper

035   Onion skin dyed eggs, Sebastian and Poppy Stubson, Ages 4 and 2; Materials: eggs, onion skins, cheesecloth, small leaves from herbs and plants, water

036   Nature Portrait, Art with Amy, Brookline, MA; Materials: canvas, paint, found materials in nature

037   Nature Weaving, Susan Schwake's Art Lab students. Materials: branches from a fallen tree, yarn, jute, yarn and assorted found nature objects

038   Autumnal leaf decoration, Sebastian Stubson, Age 4; Materials: leaves, wax paper, newsprint and iron with mom's help!

039   Exploring the Environment, Brandon Chapman, Age 3 with Artist Amy Popely, Essex, United Kingdom; Materials: paint and grass on canvas

040   Tree Slice Wreath, Saya, Age 7; Materials: cut tree branches and paint

041   Moose and Fox Ornaments, Sebastian and Poppy Stubson, Ages 4 and 2; Materials: applesauce, cinnamon, cookie cutters, and baking sheet

042   Icicle Painting, Annika Age 8, Benjamin Age 7, Samuel Age 1; Materials: Icicle and paint

043   Snow Painting, Annika Age 8, Dominica Age 8, and Benjamin Age 8, Brookline, MA; Materials: snow and pain

44 Shell Art, Gavin Minard, Age 10; Materials: found beach shells

3. Making Art Together

Collaboration between teachers and students or parents and kids is a great way to explore the creative process with a shared goal in mind. Your canvas for creativity may be big or small—a shared drawing or an outdoor mural, working together to make something gives artists of all ages and abilities a chance to contribute their creativity to a project. In this chapter, don't miss the group of kids who painted a community bus, or the projects siblings worked on together to make with the help of their parent. Just as with a solo creation, creating a work together is half the fun. Practically speaking, collaborative art projects are a natural way to help build communication skills, emphasize sharing, and respect for individual choices and creative expressions.

045   Sea Dragon, Arts in
       Nahant with Heather
       Goodwin, Ages 4–10;
       Materials: Wood,
       recycled milk and juice
       containers, masking
       tape, and paint

046   Mosaic Tile Wall for
       Outdoor Classroom,
       Sunshine Academy
       Pre-K, Brookline, MA,
       Ages 4–5;
       Materials: Wall tiles,
       cardboard, cement
       and grout

047 Van Gogh Inspired Starry Night, Phoenix School Students, Salem, MA
Ages 7–12; Materials: Insulation board and acrylic paint

048 Spider Web, PEM Pals Ages 5 and under, Peabody Essex Museum, Salem, MA;
Materials: colored masking tape

049 Extra Monsters for What's Under the Bed group project, Nancy Dapkiewicz's
"Creative Vacation: Fantasty, Myth and Magic" summer art students in grades
4–6, Massachusetts College of Art and Design, Boston, MA; Materials: cardboard
and markers

050 What's Under the Bed group project, Nancy Dapkiewicz's "Creative Vacation:
Fantasty, Myth and Magic"summer art students in grades 4–6, Massachusetts
College of Art and Design, Boston, MA; Materials: cardboard, paint and
miscellaneous found materials

051   Machine Collaboration, Naomi Ikeda, Age 5 and Iluska Ikeda; Materials: pencil, watercolor paper, brush, sharpie, and watercolors

052   Dinosaur Mural Sunshine Academy Preschool, Brookline, MA, Age 3; Materials: butcher block paper, construction paper, crayon, paint, pasta noodles dyed with food coloring, colored wood scraps, paint sample cards, and glue

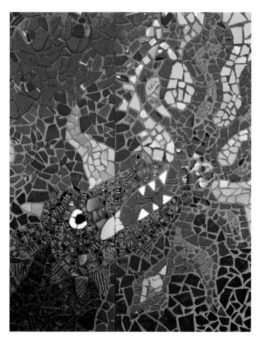

053   Four Elements—Fire, 4th year, Stadt Schule (Elementary School), Bad Oldesloe, Germany, Age 10 with artist Siobhann Tarr; Materials: broken ceramic tiles, plates, vases, cups, tile adhesive, and grout

054   Mosaic Hopscotch 4th year Class, Klaus-Groth Elementary School, Bad Oldesloe, Germany, Age 9–10, with artist Siobhann Tarr; Materials: glass mosaic tiles, tile adhesive and grout

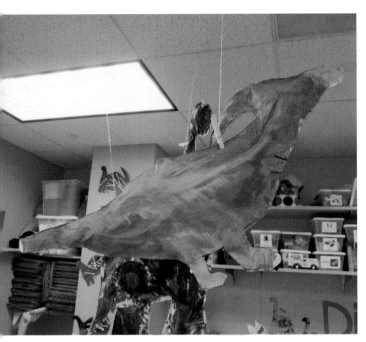

055   3-D Dinosaurs, Sunshine Academy Toddler Program, Brookline, MA:
Materials: Butcher paper, paint

056   3-D Dinosaurs, Sunshine Academy Toddler Program, Brookline, MA;
Materials: Butcher paper, paint

057   Jackson Pollack Inspired Collage, Sunshine Academy Pre-K Program,
Brookline, MA; Materials: butcher paper, paintbrushes and paint

058   Giant Globe, Sunshine Academy Pre-K Program, Brookline, MA;
Materials: papier-mache, paint, and rope

059   Cardboard Sculpture, Maker Lounge Cardboard Challenge, Peabody Essex Museum, Salem, MA; Materials: cardboard and painter's tape

060   Dragon, The Phoenix School students, Salem, MA Ages 5-12 Materials: cardboard boxes, paper cups and construction paper

061   Driftwood fish sculpture. Arts in Nahant with Heather Goodwin, Ages 5-12. Materials: driftwood painted with acrylics; frame made from pine and fisherman's net, acrylic paint.

062   3-D Octopus, Sunshine Academy Preschool Program, Brookline, MA; Materials: Butcher paper, paint

063   Beware of the Shark!, Sunshine Academy Pre-K Program, Brookline, MA;
Materials: Butcher paper, paint

064   Nahant Council on Aging Bus, Art in Nahant with Heather Goodwin, Ages 5-15.
Materials: Bus, Rustoleum paints

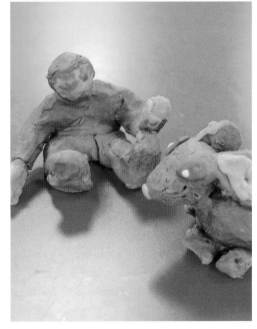

065   Big Fish, Artists in PEM Pals, Ages 5 and under, at the Peabody Essex Museum.
Materials: Kraft paper, construction paper, crayons and markers

066   A Mouse and His Boy, Anya (mouse) Age 10 and
Olivia (boy) Age 11, The Phoenix School,
Salem, MA; Materials: plasticine modeling clay

4. Mixed Media and Collage

When artists combine a range of materials and artistic processes to express themselves in creative form it is typically known as mixed media. When gluing and paper is involved, the resulting art work is often called a collage. A mashup of materials and techniques can lead to truly individual creations and it's exhilarating to observe how kids invent new ways to express themselves. As young artists become more skilled and adept with all kinds of art materials and approaches to creative expression, their potential for innovation and expressing both abstract and literal ideas multiplies. Don't miss some of the incredible mixed-media self-portraits in this chapter and the deep and meaningful worlds created in 2d with paper, paint, markers and more.

067   Owl Postage Stamp Collage, Leila Gridley, Age 8; Materials: Postage stamp, oil pastels, watercolor and felt-tip markers

068   Collaged Pages, Stephen Hully, Age 3; Materials: paper, watercolor paints, oil pastels, paper.

069   Flower Collage, Leila Gridley, Age 8; Materials: Flower cut out from magazine pages, felt center, and felt grass against watercolor background

070   I Love Bugs! Lana, Age 5; Materials: cardboard, paper, polymer clay, rope, fabric

071   Cow in Grass, Jack Owain Billowitz, Age 5; Materials: Pencil, permanent markers, water color pencils, water soluble crayons, watercolor markers, paint, fabric and paper scraps.

072   Cat Collage, Leila Gridley, Age 8; Materials: Fabric, tongue depressor, poker chip, pine tree branch and ribbons arranged on a piece of a cardboard

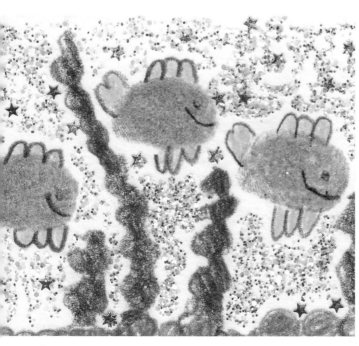

073   Fingerprint Fishes, Leila Gridley, Age 8; Materials: paint, pencil, glitter on paper

074   Spider's Web, Violet Doyle Age 3; Materials: Wax crayon, liquid water color, upcycled crochet, glue, pipe cleaners, google eyes, and pom-poms

075   The Letter A, 3D Font Design, Larchmont Charter School, Fifth Grade, Los Angeles, CA, Age 10–11; Materials: erasers in a box

076   Hope, 3D Font Design, Larchmont Charter School, Fifth Grade, Los Angeles, CA, Age 10–11; Materials: buttons and clothespins

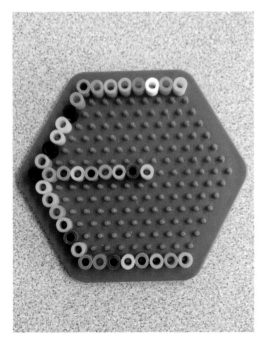

077   The Letter E, 3D Font Design, Larchmont Charter School, Fifth Grade, Los Angeles, CA, Age 10–11; Materials: Plastic pegs

078   Magazine Collage, Naomi Ikeda, Age 5; Materials: Old magazines, catalogues, and junk mail, glue, white background paper, and black fine permanent markers

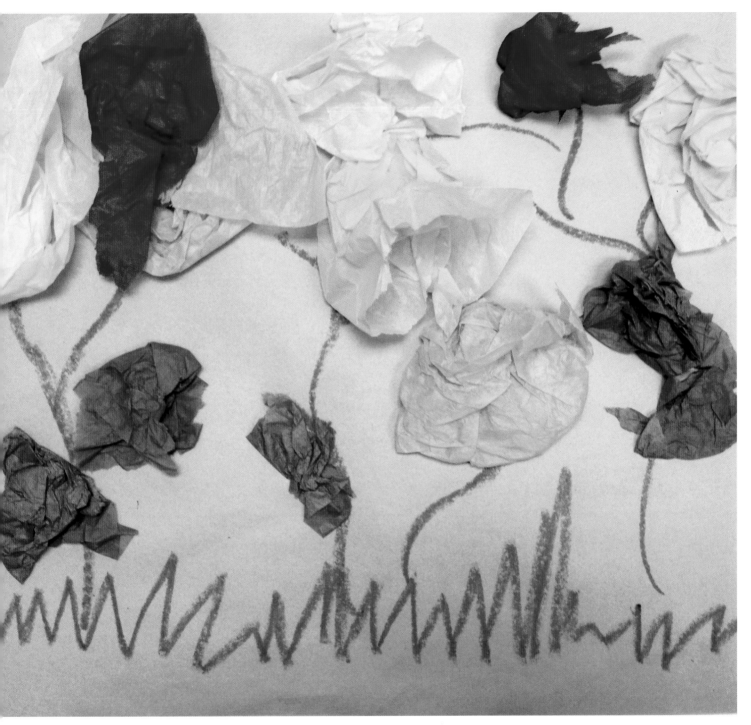

Tissue Paper Garden, Artists in PEM Pals, Ages 5 and under, at the Peabody Essex Museum;
Materials: tissue paper, construction paper, crayon, and glue.

080   Self Portrait Collage, Sarah, Age 11;
Materials: paper, fabric, foam sheets and yarn

081   Self Portrait Collage, Sherry X., Age 11;
Materials: paper, fabric, buttons,
found materials

082   Portrait Collage, Susan Schwake's Art Lab
students; Materials: Newspaper, glue,
watercolor pencils and watercolor paper

083   Lion, Kyle Browne's art students, Boys and Girls
Club, Salem, MA ages 8–11; Materials: card
board and found objects including paper,
stickers, cut magazines

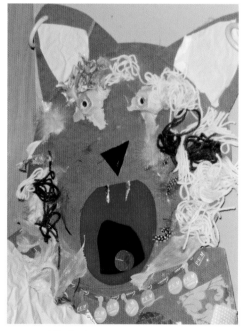

084   Big Cat, Kyle Browne's art students, Boys and
Girls Club, Salem, MA ages 8–11;
Materials: cardboard and found objects
including paper, stickers, cut magazines

085   Joy, Susan Schwake's Art Lab students;
Materials: Acrylic paint, newspaper on
canvas board

086 Newfound Lake Collage, Stellan, Age 4; Materials: Paper, felt, post-it notes, pipe cleaners, reflective paper and colored tape

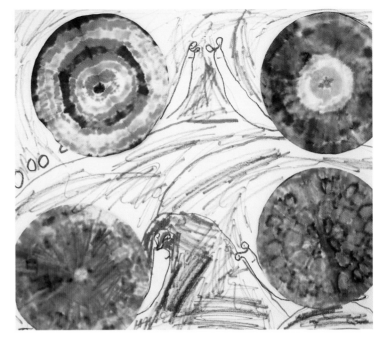

087 Snails, Artist in Brandie Pettus' Create Art With Me Art Classes, Age 9; Materials: coffee filter, sprayed watercolors, markers, paper

088 Map Collage, Susan Schwake's Art Lab students; Materials: Old maps, various papers, markers and glue

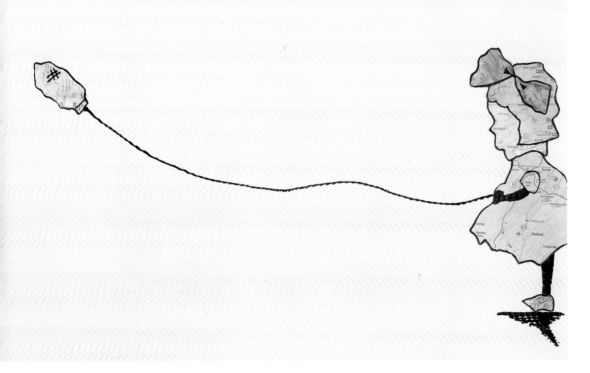

089 Bugs, Susan Schwake's Art Lab students; Materials: contact paper for bug shapes, colored pencils, markers on wooden panel

090 Family Quilts, Susan Schwake's Art Lab students; Materials: oil pastels, watercolors on paper

091 Painted Photograph Portrait, Susan Schwake's Art Lab students; Materials: Acrylic paint on canvas board, printed image on decal paper, acrylic medium

092 Larger than Life, Susan Schwake's Art Lab students; Materials: Magazines, glue on poster paper

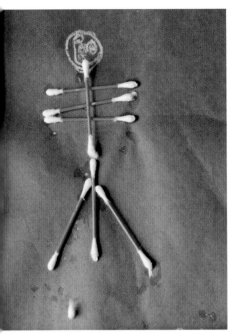

093   Skeleton, Stellan, Age 4; Materials: construction paper, white crayon and cotton swabs

094   Parrot, Susan Schwake's Art Lab students; Materials: pencils and watercolors on watercolor paper

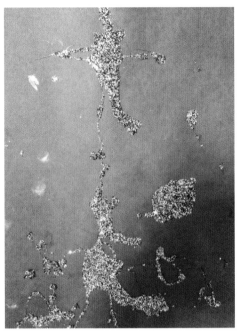

095   Fireworks, Mason Age 4; Materials: construction paper, glitter and glue

096   Surfboard, Stellan Age 4; Materials: pre-cut surfboard shape from cardboard, cut paper, markers and glue

097   Woven Collage, Susan Schwake's Art Lab students; Materials: Cardboard, assorted yarns, feathers, fabric scraps and tape

098   Tri-color Portrait , Susan Schwake's Art Lab students; Materials: Oil pastels in black, white and red; drawing paper, paper scraps, and markers

099   Fabric Collage, Susan Schwake's Art Lab students;
Materials: Wooden board, paint markers, fabric
scraps and glue

100   Paper Mache Minis, Susan Schwake's Art Lab students;
Materials: Newspaper, white paper towels, colored tissue paper, and waxed paper

101   Wallpaper Collage, Susan Schwake's Art Lab
students; Materials: wallpaper samples, straws
for painting the flower stems, tissue paper and
cardstock

102   Tape Flag, Susan Schwake's Art Lab students;
Materials: Colored tape, watercolor paint and cardstock paper

103   Aquarium, Stellan Age 4; Materials: paper, aquarium props, cut paper, markers and plastic bag

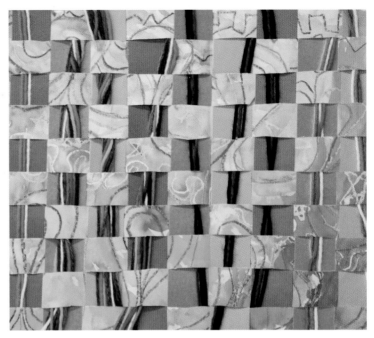

104   Paper and Yarn Weaving, Amy Aker's 1st grade art class, Chelmsford Public Schools, MA; Materials: paper, crayon and watercolor, acrylic yarn

105   Connect the Dots, Susan Schwake's Art Lab students; Materials: black permanent marker, oil pastels, watercolors and cardstock paper

106   Passport Project, Joseph Luongo's 1st grade Art Class, Malden, MA Public Schools; Materials: Printed images, consruction paper, and crayons

107   Oil Pastel Collage, Susan Schwake's Art Lab students; Materials: Magazine scraps, oil pastels, watercolors and cardstock

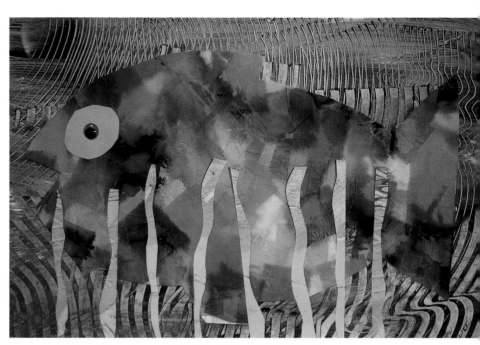

108   Fish, Joseph Luongo's 1st grade Art Class, Malden, MA Public Schools; Materials: oaktag, tissue paper squares, scrap paper, wallpaper and glue

109   Front Page Portrait, Joseph Luongo's 1st grade Art Class, Malden, MA Public Schools; Materials: Printed photograph, newspaper, consruction paper, oil pastels

110   Dragon, Joseph Luongo's 1st grade Art Class, Malden, MA Public Schools; Materials: oaktag, tissue paper squares, scrap paper, wallpaper and glue.

11 Big Fish, Little Fish, Joseph Luongo's 1st grade Art Class, Malden, MA Public Schools; Materials: Block printed paper, colored paper, colored pencils and glue

112 Tesselation Self-Portrait, Joseph Luongo's 7th grade Art Class, Malden, MA Public Schools; Materials: Styrofoam printing plate and screen printing inks, cut construction paper

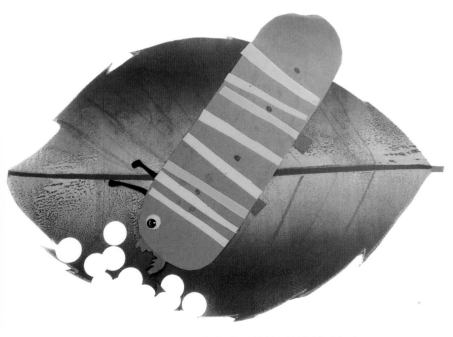

13 Caterpillar Print, Joseph Luongo's 1st grade Art Class, Malden, MA Public Schools; Materials: Ink, brayer, construction paper, hole punch and glue

114 Grand Theft Auto, Joseph Luongo's 8th grade Art Class, Malden, MA Public Schools; Materials: Paste paper, and inkjet image transfer

115 Peacock, Joseph Luongo's 6th grade Art Class, Malden, MA Public Schools; Materials: Cut paper, crayons, markers, and gel pens

116 Snake, Joseph Luongo's 6th grade Art Class, Malden, MA Public Schools; Materials: Cut paper, crayons, markers, and gel pens

117 New York, Joseph Luongo's 7th grade Art Class, Malden, MA Public Schools; Materials: Photo copied images, cut paper, and airbrushed stenciles

118 Cat, Joseph Luongo's 6th grade Art Class, Malden, MA Public Schools; Materials: Cut paper, crayons, markers, and gel pens

119　Passport Project, Joseph Luongo's 1st grade Art Class, Malden, MA Public Schools; Materials: Printed images, consruction paper, and crayons

120　The Dog At My Homework, Joseph Luongo's 3rd grade Art Class, Malden, MA Public Schools; Materials: Wallpaper, paper, photograph, crayons, colored pencils, markers

121　Keith Haring Inspired Portrait, Joseph Luongo's 2nd grade Art Class, Malden, MA Public Schools; Materials: Paper, gel pens, markers, colored pencils, oil pastels, tempera paint applied on the sole of the student's shoe and printed onto the paper

122　The Lost Cat, James, Age 8, The Phoenix School, Salem, MA; Materials: Tissue Paper, paper, markers, and glue

123   Giraffe, Gabrielle, Age 8 and Ella, Age 5, The Phoenix School, Salem, MA; Materials: foam core, construction paper, and paper fasteners as joints

124   Snowman, Sunshine Academy Toddler Program, Brookline, MA; Materials: butcher paper, cotton balls, pom-poms, paint, and reflective poster board.

125   Flower, Sunshine Academy Preschool Program Brookline, MA; Materials: seeds, glue, construction paper, and markers

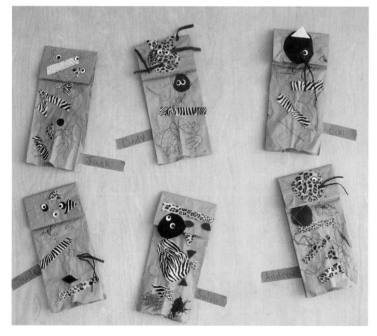

126   Paper Bag Animals, Sunshine Academy Toddler Program, Brookline, MA; Materials: brown paper bags, patterned paper and fabric, markers, and glue.

127   Baaaa, Sunshine Academy Toddler Proram, Brookline, MA; Materials: Contact paper, cotton balls, and markers

28   Cameo Pin, Susan Schwake's Art Lab students;
      Materials: cardstock, beads, glue, felt, and pin backing

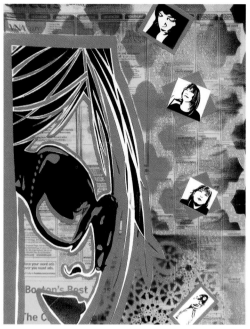

129   Self Portrait, Joseph Luongo's 7th grade Art Class,
Malden, MA Public Schools; Materials: Photo
copied images, cut paper, and airbrushed stenciles

130   Self Portrait, Joseph Luongo's 7th grade Art Class, Malden, MA Public Schools;
Materials: Photocopied images, cut paper, and airbrushed stenciles

131   My Heart, Joseph Luongo's 8th grade Art Class,
Malden, MA Public Schools; Materials: Paste paper
and inkjet image transfer

132   We Are Phoenix! The Phoenix School, Salem, MA; Materials: cut out paper people,
construction paper and yarn

133 Pizza, Sunshine Academy Preschool Program, Brookline, MA;
Materials: butcher paper, construction paper and paint.

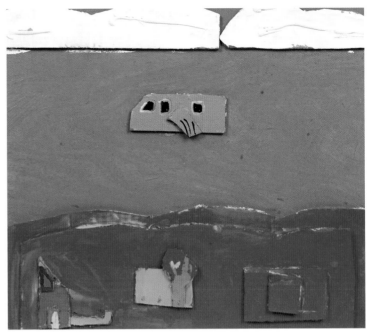

134 Cardboard Collage, Susan Schwake's Art Lab students; Materials: Assorted
cardboard pieces, acrylic paint, wood panel, glue

135 The Science of Salamanders, Maddie, Age 7, The Phoenix School, Salem, MA;
Materials: Paper, markers, and clothespin

136 Batik Landscape, Susan Schwake's Art Lab students;
Materials: Batik effect created using glue on fabric, painted with acrylic paint

5. Paint Projects

Paint is such an exciting and essential tool in the young artist's toolbox. Paint may be used as a primary medium to illustrate a landscape or as an embellishment to sculpture, or enhanced with glitter or shaving cream for a totally new effect. Experiment with how paint is applied by painting with a pencil eraser, leaves, or even ice cubes. There are a wide variety of types of paint available but tempera, acrylic, and watercolor paints are among the easiest to mix, apply, and clean up. New technologies are emerging quickly and changing even standard paints—you can now use conductive paints to create interactive murals or greeting cards!

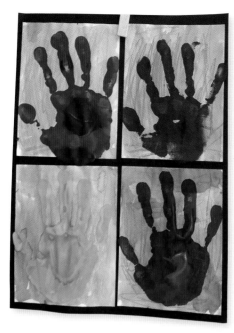

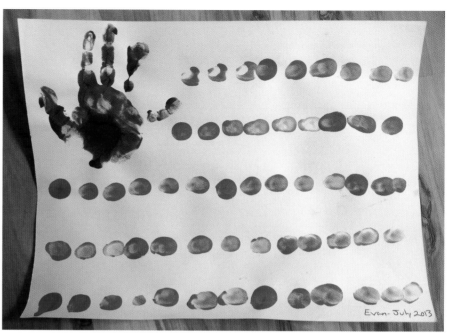

137   Handprint Pop Art, Ms, Warthen's Kindergarten Art Class; Materials: Crayon, watercolor and tempera paints.

138   Finger Painted American Flag, Evan and Owen, Ages 3 and 1; Materials: Paper and finger paint

139   Self Portrait, Simone Skiles, Age 8; Materials: Paint on kraft paper

140   Paint exploration, home school preschoolers Baraboo, WI, Age 3; Materials: long mirror, shaving cream, food coloring, paint brushes, ground or table covering, wash cloths for clean up

41   Stained Glass Hearts, Grace Campbell, Age 4, Materials: Coffee filters and watercolor paint

142   Painted Pots, Calvin Vantrease, Age 3, Materials: Terracotta clay pots, tempera paint and polyurethane

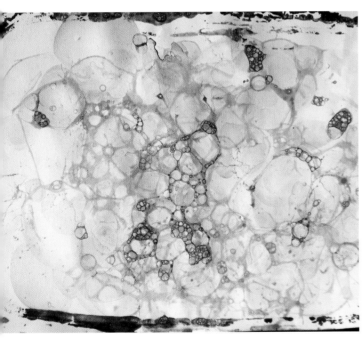

43   Bubble Painting, Stellan, Age 4, Materials: paper, soap, water and acrylic paint

144   My name is... Stellan, Age 4, Materials: Wax resist technique using white crayon and watercolor paints

145 Finger Painted Easter Eggs, Evan and Owen, Ages 3 and 1; Materials: Hardboiled eggs and paint

146 Mixed-Media Painting, Alexandra Marie Hall, Age 9; Materials: acrylics, recycled paper cut out for flower

147 My Mom, Alexandra Marie Hall, Age 9; Materials: acrylic paint

148 Color Wheel Star, Artists in the Art Link program, ages 6–11, Peabody Essex Museum; Materials: white cotton rags dipped in paint

149 Lazy Susan Drip Painting, Artists in the Art Link program, ages 6–11, Peabody Essex Museum; Materials: lazy Susan wheel, cardstock paper, squeeze bottles and paint

150 Surreal Ocean Creature, Robea Patrowicz's 2nd grade art students, Andover, MA Public Schools; Materials: watercolor paper, watercolor paints, crayons, markers, pencils

51 Mixed Media Painting, Alexandra Marie Hall, Age 9;
Materials: acrylic paint, brushes, credit card to scrape paint.

152   A Painting of Music, Alexandra Marie Hall, Age 9;
Materials: oil pastel as resist and watercolor.

153   Watercolor Pages, Stephen Hully, Age 3; Materials: paper, watercolor paints and crayons

154   Homage to Picasso, Alexandra Marie Hall, Age 9;
Materials:acrylic paint on paper

155   Painted Book Pages, Stephen Hully, Age 3; Materials: paper, oil pastels, colored pencil, watercolor paints

156   Seashell Painting, Caitlin Corrigan; Materials; Paint on paper

157   Campfire Color Mixing, Stellan, age 4; Materials: orange, red and yellow paint on paper with tissue paper.

158   Pumpkins, Elsa, Age 1; Materials: paint on paper

159   Still Life, Spencer, Age 6; Materials: oil pastels, blended with baby oil and cotton swab; watercolor paint wash

160 Exploring the Galaxy, Isabella Riva, Age 4;
Materials: watercolor on paper

161 Brave the Stage, Nathan, Age 21/2; Materials: acrylic paint on canvas

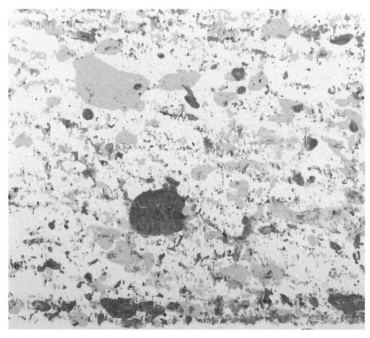

162 Marble Painting, Jesper 18 months; Materials: paint on paper

163 Paint Pouring, Families at Studio Discovery Program, Peabody Essex Museum,
Salem, MA. Wood base and wood boards, paint poured over the structure.

164 Paint and Ink Painting, Susan Schwake's Art Lab students;
Materials: India ink, acrylic paint, straw to blow ink on paper on canvas board

165 Pasta Painting, Charley, 18 months with Artist Amy Popely, Essex,
United Kingdom; Materials: paint, uncooked pasta and canvas board

166 Op Art, Susan Schwake's Art Lab students;
Materials: Watercolors, oil pastels, and drawing paper

167 Owl, Elsa, 19 months; Materials: paint on paper

168   Seascape, Susan Schwake's Art Lab students; Materials: Charcoal and watercolors on watercolor paper

169   Paint Exploration, Charley 18 months with Artist Amy Popely, Essex, United Kingdom; Materials: paint on canvas

170   Circle Painting, Susan Schwake's Art Lab students ; Materials: Acrylic paint and construction paper

171   Expressionist Style Portrait, Joseph Luongo's 4th grade Art Class, Malden, MA Public Schools; Materials: Painted paper, colored paper and wallpaper collaged with painted portrait

172   Expressionist Style Portrait, Joseph Luongo's 4th grade Art Class, Malden, MA Public Schools; Materials: Painted paper, colored paper and wallpaper collaged with painted portrait

173   Where We Live, Susan Schwake's Art Lab students; Materials: Watercolors, oil pastels, black marker, and canvas board

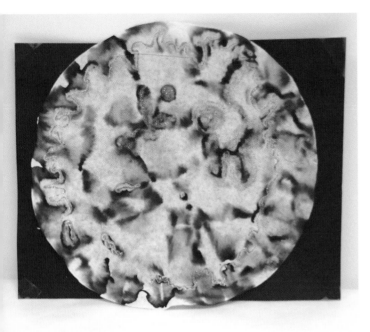

174 Blue Swirls, Stellan, Age 4; Materials: colored paper, coffee filter, paint, and glitter glue

175 Paint Exploration, PEM Pals, Ages 5 and under, Peabody Essex Museum, Salem, MA; Materials: Acrylic paint in plastic bags on a light box.

176 Color Mixing Challenge, Susan Schwake's Art Lab students; Materials: Watercolors, brushes and cardstock paper

177 Cotton Ball Color, Susan Schwake's Art Lab students; Materials: Tempera paints, cotton balls, cotton swabs, white cardstock paper

178   Spray Bottle Painting, Susan Schwake's Art Lab students;
Materials: Watercolors, spray bottle with water, watercolor paper

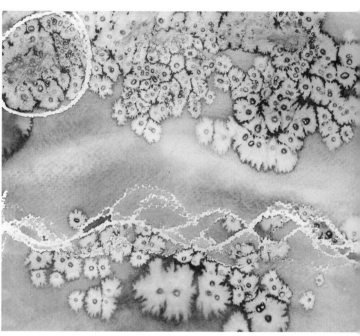

179   Watercolor and Pastel Painting Susan Schwake's Art Lab students;
Materials: White oil pastel, watercolors, salt, small sponge,
and watercolor paper

180   Ice Painting, Susan Schwake's Art Lab students; Materials: ice cubes made with
food coloring, craft sticks and paper

181   Splatter Art, Susan Schwake's Art Lab students; Materials: Watercolors,
brushes and cardstock paper

182   Paint Exploration, Sunshine Academy Toddler Program, Brookline, MA;
Materials: Shaving cream, paint, and plastic cups

183   Starch Painting, Sunshine Academy Toddler Program, Brookline, MA;
Materials: paint and cornstarch on paper

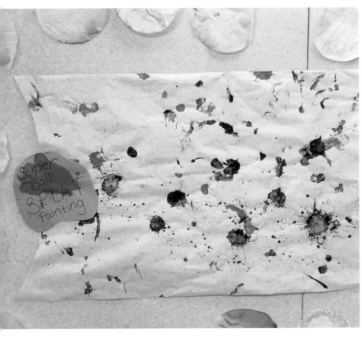

184   Superballs, Sunshine Academy Preschool Program, Brookline, MA;
Materials: paper, paint, superballs dipped in paint and bounced on the paper

185   Texture Painting, Sunshine Academy Toddler Program, Brookline, MA;
Materials: found objects dipped in paint on paper

186   Bathtub Art, Samuel, Age 4, Brookline, MA; Materials: paint on ceramic tile

187   Maine Tree, Jesse, Age 7; Materials: canvas board and acrylic paint

188   Vroom, vroom! Sunshine Academy Toddler Program, Brookline, MA; Materials: Toy cars and paint on butcher paper

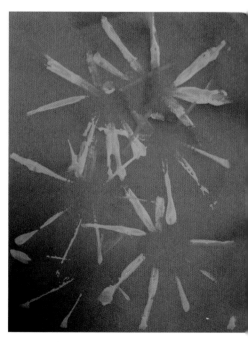

189   Fireworks, Artists in PEM Pals, Ages 5 and under, at the Peabody Essex Museum. Materials: Pipe cleaners dipped in paint and stamped on construction paper

Still Life, Jesse, Age 7; Materials: Stretched canvas and acrylic paint

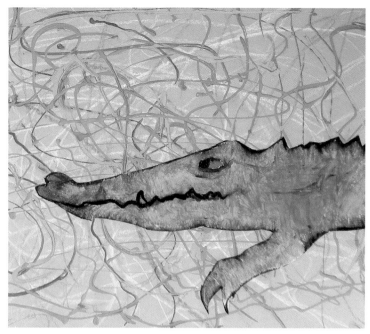

191   Crocodile, Joseph Luongo's 4th grade Art Class, Malden, MA Public Schools;
Materials: Paint squirted on the paper with glue containers and cut paper

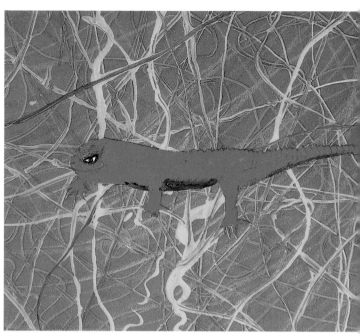

192   Iguana, Joseph Luongo's 4th grade Art Class, Malden, MA Public Schools;
Materials: Paint squirted on the paper with glue containers and cut paper

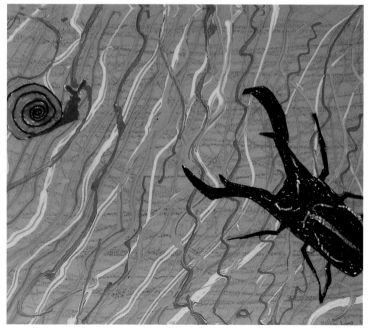

193   Snail, Joseph Luongo's 4th grade Art Class, Malden, MA Public Schools;
Materials: Paint squirted on the paper with glue containers and cut paper

194   Snake, Joseph Luongo's 4th grade Art Class, Malden, MA Public Schools;
Materials: Paint squirted on the paper with glue containers and cut paper

195   Turtles, Joseph Luongo's 4th grade Art Class, Malden, MA Public Schools; Materials: Paint squirted on the paper with glue containers and cut paper

196   Shark, Joseph Luongo's 4th grade Art Class, Malden, MA Public Schools; Materials: Paint squirted on the paper with glue containers and cut paper

197   Graffiti Style Painting, Joseph Luongo's 8th grade Art Class, Malden, MA Public Schools; Materials: Paper, airbrush paint and stencils, colored pencils

198   Graffiti Style Painting, Joseph Luongo's 8th grade Art Class, Malden, MA Public Schools; Materials: Paper, airbrush paint and stencils, colored pencils

199 Dot Art, Ramon, Age 10, The Phoenix School, Salem, MA; Materials: watercolors on construction paper

200 Inspired by Seurat's Bathers at Asnieries, Students at The Phoenix School Salem, MA Ages 8–12; Materials: Acyclic paint on foam core

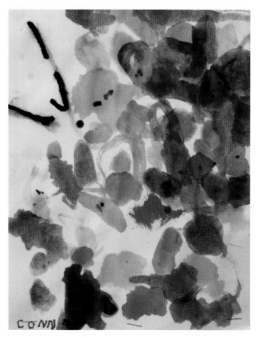

201 Dot Art, Connor, Age 5, The Phoenix School, Salem, MA; Materials: pipe cleaners, watercolors on paper

202 Salem Landmarks, Students at The Phoenix School Salem, MA Ages 5–14; Materials: acrylic paint on luan

203 Dot Art, Mayan, Age 12, The Phoenix School, Salem, MA;
Materials: watercolors on paper

204 Ball Painting, Sunshine Academy Infant Program, Brookline, MA;
Materials: pain, paper and plastic balls

205 Geeked out on Greeks Painting, Bianca Falcone in Nancy Dapkiewicz's
grade 6 art class at Stoneham Middle School, Stoneham, MA;
Materials: watercolor on paper.

206 Geeked out on Greeks Painting. Cameron Gilmartin in Nancy Dapkiewicz's
grade 6 art class at Stoneham Middle School, Stoneham, MA;
Materials: watercolor on paper.

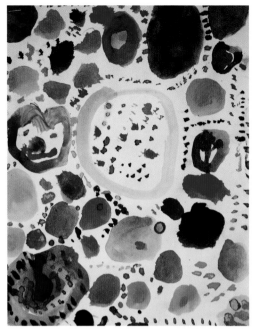

211   Dot Art, Jed, Age 7, The Phoenix School,
Salem, MA; Materials: watercolors on paper

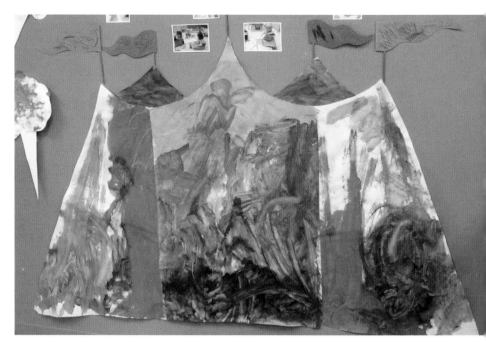

212   Circus Tent, Sunshine Academy Pre-K Program, Brookline, MA;
Materials: Paper, construction paper and paint

213   Paint Exploration and Color Mixing, Sunshine
Academy Toddler Program, Brookline, MA;
Materials: Masking tape, paint, plastic bags

214   Underwater Mural, Sunshine Academy Preschool Program, Brookline, MA; Butcher paper painted by student
and cut by the teachers for the seaweed and water, construction paper sea creatures

215   Basketball, Sunshine Academy Toddler Program, Brookline, MA;
Materials: paper, paint, and markers, basketball dipped in paint and bounced
on the paper

216   Dirt Painting, Sunshine Academy Toddler Program, Brookline, MA;
Materials: soaked coffee grounds and construction paper

217   Food Painting, Sunshine Academy Toddler Program, Brookline, MA;
Materials: cut fruit, paint, and paper

218   Paint with your Fork, Sunshine Academy Toddler Program, Brookline, MA;
Materials: forks, spoon, paint, and paper

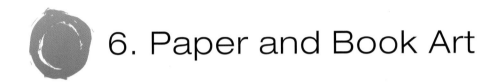

6. Paper and Book Art

How does thin, flat, two-dimensional paper become an entirely new three-dimensional form? In this chapter, explore that dramatic transformation with works including origami art, pop-ups, and creative self-made books. In addition to paper as an art material, making paper is a creative experience as well. Use found books as the basis for a sculpture or cut up old magazines and decorated paper to illustrate an image or idea on paper. The possibilities are endless and this chapter shares just a few inspiring examples.

219 Bird pop-up card, Jenna Fan, Age 9, Materials: Paper and markers

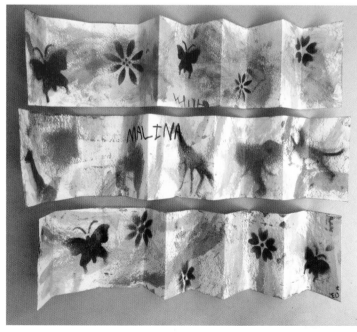

220 Self-cover accordion books, Elaine Chu's kindergarten class, Kensington, CA, Ages 5 to 6; Materials: Finger paints, rubber stamp inks, paper, stencils

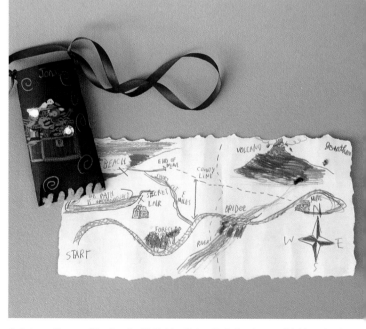

221 Treasure Map Scroll with Holder, Elaine Chu's Kensington, CA Afterschool Enrichment Program, artist Jonathan Franaszek, Age 8; Materials: color pencils, paper, ribbon, pipe cleaners, ribbon, adhesive jewels

222 Parent Portraits. Elsa, Age 2; Materials: pre-cut construction paper shapes and glue

223 Bird with Flag Wings, Alexandra Marie Hall, Age 9; Materials: crayons and paper

224 Reindeer, Alexandra and Madeline Godin, Age 5; Materials: Children's feet outlines are used to form the reindeer's head. Outline of their hands are used to create the antlers. Construction paper, glue and pom-pom

225 Origami Penguins, Family art program at the Peabody Essex Museum; Materials: origami paper

226   A House for Romare Bearden, Mrs. Bower's 3rd grade artists, Niles, MI Age 8; Materials: construction papers, magazines, and glue

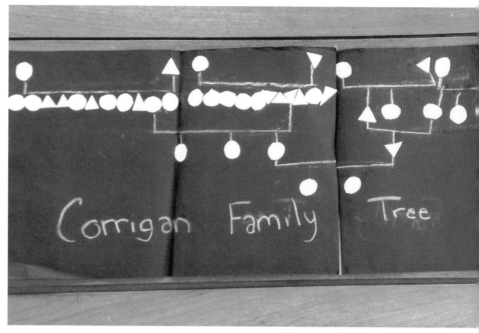

227   Paper Family Tree, Caitlin Corrigan; Materials: Construction paper, chalk

228   Handmade paper, Leila Gridley, Age 8; Materials: Pressed flowers and leaves, torn napkin pieces, and glitter

229   Earth Day Art, Johnson School Kindergarten and 1st grade students with Heather Goodwin; Materials: paper plates, tissue paper, and glue

230   Paper outfits for stuffed animals, Mae Abernathy Age 6; Materials: paper

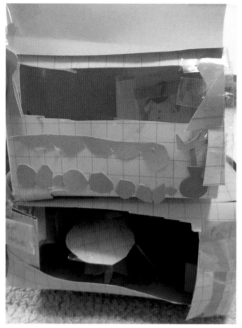

231   Paper Doll House, Lily Saeki, Age 7, Tokyo, Japan; Materials: paper

232   Bird Puppets, Asher, Age 6; Materials: matte board, watercolor and acrylic paint, handmade potato stamps, brass fasteners

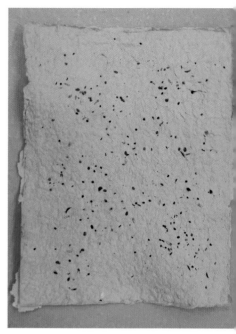

233   Plantable Seed Paper, Artists in the Art Link program, ages 6–11, Peabody Essex Museum; Materials: Paper pulp and grass seeds

234   Self Portrait, Stellan, Age 4; Materials: Cut paper and pipe cleaner

235   Windows, Kyle Browne's art students, Jamaica Plain, MA ages 5 and up; Materials: found book and collage papers

236   Book Mobile, Kyle Browne's art students, Jamaica Plain, MA ages 5 and up; Materials: found book and yarn

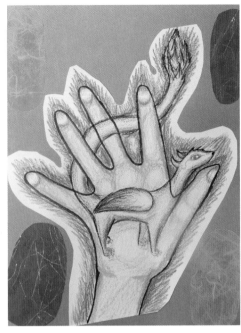

237   Tissue Paper Leaf, Artists in PEM Pals, Ages 5
and under, at the Peabody Essex Museum;
Materials: black construction paper, tissue
paper, and glue

238   Collage, Jordan Schnitzer Museum of Art,
University of Oregon afterschool program.
Construction paper, decorative paper, colored
pencil, marker

239   Self-Portrait, Susan Schwake's Art Lab
students; Materials: Tissue paper, glue and
markers on paper

240   Mushrooms, Susan Schwake's Art Lab students;
Materials: Vellum, acrylic paint, needle and t
hread, colored pencils

241   A House for Romare Bearden, Mrs. Bower's
3rd grade artists, Niles, MI Age 8;
Materials: construction papers, magazines,
and glue

242 Roots and Shoots: Local Flora Flower Collage, Artist Kyle Browne with students at Boys and Girls Club, Salem, MA Ages 7–11, Materials: Torn/ cut paper on a watercolor painted background

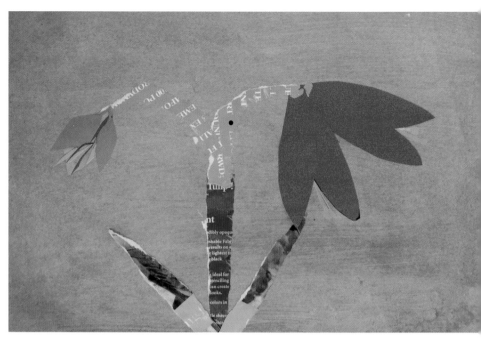

243 Roots and Shoots: Local Flora Flower Collage, Artist Kyle Browne with students at Boys and Girls Club, Salem, MA Ages 7–11, Materials: Torn and cut paper collaged onto a watercolor painted background

244 Roots and Shoots: Local Flora Flower Collage, Artist Kyle Browne with students at Boys and Girls Club, Salem, MA Ages 7–11, Materials: Torn/cut paper on a watercolor painted background

245 Roots and Shoots: Local Flora Flower Collage, Artist Kyle Browne with students at Boys and Girls Club, Salem, MA Ages 7–11, Materials: Torn and cut paper collaged onto a watercolor painted background

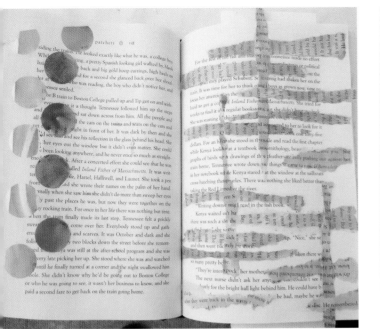

246   Pastels Page, Kyle Browne's art students, Jamaica Plain, MA ages 5 and up; Materials: found book and collage papers

247   Birch Trees, Spencer, Age 6; Materials: Paper and paint

248   Dolphin Page, Kyle Browne's art students, Jamaica Plain, MA ages 5 and up; Materials: found book, collage papers and fabrics, embellishments and markers

249   Paper Sculpture, Adalay, Age 5; Materials: construction paper

250   Tissue Paper Sculpture, Adalay, Age 5; Materials: construction paper

251   Shades of the Rainbow, Artists in PEM Pals, Ages 5 and under, at the Peabody Essex Museum; Materials: tonal scraps of paper, copy paper, and glue

252   Tissue Paper Birds, Lilly, Age 10; Materials: tissue paper, cardstock, popsicle sticks, a dowel rod, and markers

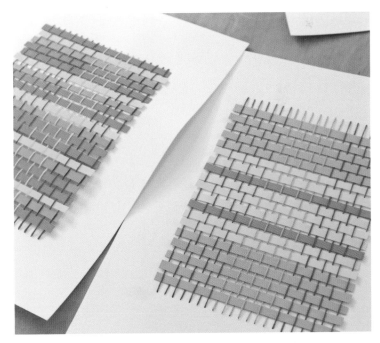

253   Woven Paper, Saya, Age 7; Materials: thread and cardstock pieces

254   Cut Paper Mask, Susan Schwake's Art Lab students; Materials: Colored copy paper and glue

255   Paper Fish, Susan Schwake's Art Lab students; Materials: Watercolors on two large sheets of heavy paper, cut in the shape of fish and stuffed with newspaper

256   Butterfly, Mason Age 4; Materials: paper, stamped paint and yarn

257   Fish, Stellan Age 4; Materials: muffin wrappers and colored paper with markers

258   Monster Art, Susan Schwake's Art Lab students; Materials: Textured designs created with oil pastel rubbed over texture plates, construction paper, watercolors on paper

259   Torn-Paper Landscape, Susan Schwake's Art Lab students; Materials: Matboard, construction paper and glue

260   Coffee Can Collage, Susan Schwake's Art Lab students; Materials: Colored paper, pencil and glue

261   Bzzz, Sunshine Academy Preschool Progam, Brookline, MA; Materials: construction paper, marker and glue

272   Dragon, Joseph Luongo's
       Kindergarten Art Class,
       Malden, MA Public
       Schools; Materials: cut
       scrap paper, wallpaper
       and glue

273   Dragon, Joseph Luongo's
       Kindergarten Art Class,
       Malden, MA Public
       Schools; Materials: cut
       scrap paper, wallpaper,
       and glue

Journeys of the
KIT-KAT CLUB

NEW YORK
D. APPLETON AND COMPANY
1908

QUEEN ELIZABETH

Steampunk Assemblage Book, Georgiana Carmack, Age 10, Wendy LaGreen and Marka Burns' classroom at Eldorado Emerson School, Orange, CA.;
Materials: Vintage book, metal toy rockets, wooden tassels, cell phone cover, metal door knobs

275 Autumn Star Book, Nikola Susec, in a creative writing and illustration camp taught by Arthurina Fears, Museum Educator, at the Jordan Schnitzer Museum of Art, University of Oregon; Materials: watercolor paper, watercolor, ink, pencil, decorative paper

276 Dot Art, Ellie, Age 9, The Phoenix School, Salem, MA; Materials: CD, buttons, watercolor paints, plastic lid and paper

277 Family Crest, created in Nancy Dapkiewicz's grade 6 art class at Stoneham Middle School, Stoneham, MA; Materials: cut paper and glue

278 Family Crest, created in Nancy Dapkiewicz's grade 6–8 art class at Stoneham Middle School, Stoneham, MA; Materials: cut paper and glue

279 Family Crest, created in Nancy Dapkiewicz's grade 6 art class at Stoneham Middle School, Stoneham, MA; Materials: cut paper and glue

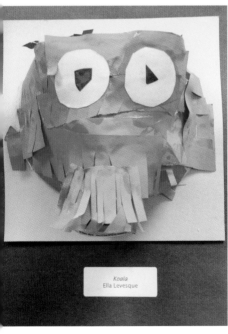

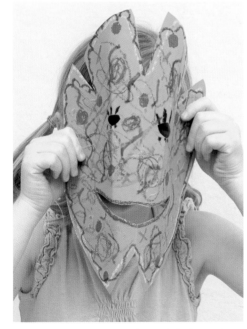

280 Koala, Ella Levesque, Age 4, The Phoenix School, Salem ,MA; Materials: construction paper and paper cup

281 Paper Collage, Susan Schwake's Art Lab students; Materials: Origami paper glued on mat board

282 Paper Mask, Susan Schwake's Art Lab students; Materials: Oil pastel on cardstock paper, yarn

7. Printmaking and Stamping

Professional printmakers can spend years perfecting a single printmaking technique while also making their own unique papers to print on. Although this may sound daunting, the world of printmaking is incredibly diverse and unlimited as a form of creative expression and is in fact very accessible to kids. Young artists can explore the basic forms of prints through simple stamping with foam shapes or even cut food! As they grow and develop they can discover more complicated, multi-step processes with a variety of printmaking techniques. In this chapter, see examples of printmaking such as the classic kid-friendly Styrofoam printing plate technique, and discover how glue can be used to create abstract printing blocks.

283   Bell Pepper Shamrock Stamps, Evan and Owen, Ages 3 and 1; Materials: Halved bell peppers and paint

284   Construction Scene, Susan Schwake's Art Lab students; Materials: palette and brayer, water-based ink on paper

285   Leaf print, Artists in PEM Pals, Ages 0–5 at the Peabody Essex Museum; Materials: Cardstock, paint and tree leaves

286   String Art, Susan Schwake's Art Lab students; Materials: Acrtylic paint, cotton string dipped in paint on paper

295 287   Animals and More! Jenna and Coby Fan, ages 9 and 11; Materials: Water-soluble block printing inks, paper, rubber (for carving)

288   Screened Flower, Susan Schwake's Art Lab students; Materials: Home-made screen using embroidery hoop and screening fabric, glue, wax paper, acyrlic paint, and textile medium

297 289   Cardboard Print, Susan Schwake's Art Lab students; Materials: Corrugated cardboard piecescut and glued to cardstock; inked with block printing ink and printed on blue printing paper

290   Mixed-Media Print, Susan Schwake's Art Lab students; Materials: Gelatin plate, block printing ink and found objects printed on paper

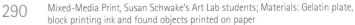

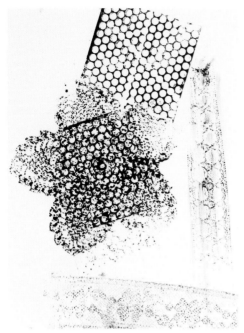

304   Lace Print, Susan Schwake's Art Lab students; Materials: Assorted laces, water-based block printing ink, brayer and ink tray

305   Sand and Glue Painting, Susan Schwake's Art Lab students; Materials: Oil pastels, sand, cotton batting, glue and cardstock

306   Letter Print, Susan Schwake's Art Lab students; Materials: Foam letter stamps, paint and cardstock paper

307   Mask Inspired Portrait, Joseph Luongo's 8th grade Art Class, Malden, MA Public Schools; Materials: Chipboard and oaktag used to create a printing plate replicating an image drawn by the student, block printing inks, brayer and colored paper

308   Mask Inspired Portrait, Joseph Luongo's 8th grade Art Class, Malden, MA Public Schools; Materials: Chipboard and oaktag used to create a printing plate replicating an image drawn by the student, block printing inks, brayer and colored paper

309   Snow Leopard, Joseph Luongo's 5th grade Art Class, Malden, MA Public Schools; Materials: Styrofoam used to create printing plates; two phase printing using block printing inks.

310 Zebra, Joseph Luongo's 5th grade Art Class, Malden, MA Public Schools; Materials: Styrofoam used to create printing plates; two phase printing using block printing inks.

311 Hedgehog, Joseph Luongo's 5th grade Art Class, Malden, MA Public Schools; Materials: Styrofoam used to create printing plates; two phase printing using block printing inks

8. Recycled and Upcycled

Look no further than your recycling bin to stock art materials! Cardboard, egg cartons, and even plastic cups are a great starting point for creative projects. Large, discarded cardboard boxes can take on new life as a play house or train and a tin can becomes a robot. Discover how some young artists saved trash from our landfills by offering cast aside materials a second chance.

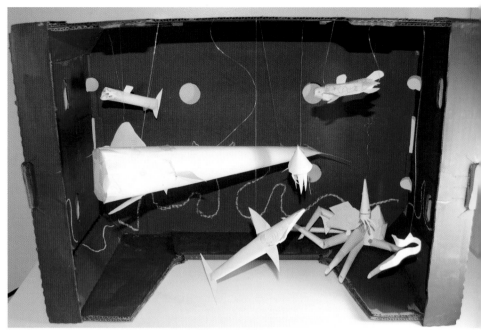

312   Hungry Cardboard Turkey, Erin Snyder with Evan and Owen, Age 3 and 1; Materials: cardboard box, paper, and glue

313   Undersea Creatures, Dylan Abernathy, Age 10; Materials: Recycled boxes, paper, tape and fishing line

314   Lily's Art Museum, Lily Saeki, Age 7, Tokyo, Japan; Materials: origami paper, toilet paper rolls, recycled packing foam and an old cardboard box

315   Save the Rhino (Wearing a Camouflage Blanket), Isabelle, Age 12, The Phoenix School, Salem, MA; Materials: Plastic bottle, construction paper and packing tape

316   Rocket, Stellan age 4; Materials: recycled mailing tube, aluminum foil, colored masking tape, foam, and pipe cleaners

317   Fairy House, Elena McDonald, Age 11, Materials: recycled wooden boards, old dish rack, popsicle sticks, fabric and felt scraps, string, shoe laces and old toys

318   Animal Puppets, Artists, Age 4–16, from Rebecca Szeto's makeSHIFT Creativity Workshop; Materials: toilet paper rolls, felt scraps, eyes, and glue

319   Fish, Alexandra Godin, Age 4; Materials: paper plates and paint

325 Giant Butterflies,
Students at The
Phoenix School,
Salem, MA;
Materials: pizza boxes,
acrylic paint,
construction paper,
colored paper

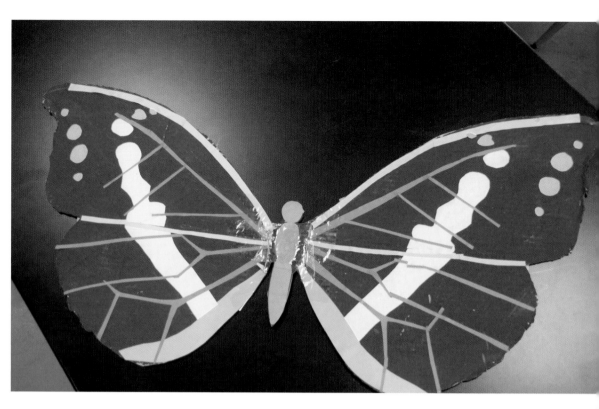

326 Giant Butterflies,
Students at The
Phoenix School,
Salem, MA;
Materials: pizza boxes,
acrylic paint,
construction paper,
colored paper

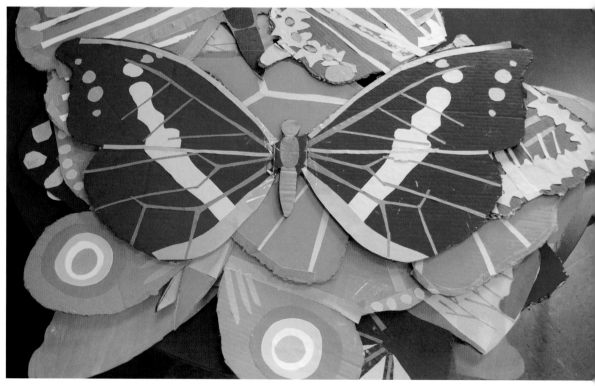

327 Painted lanterns, Arts in Nahant with Heather Goodwin, Ages 5–12;
Materials: recycled juice and milk containers, masking tape, and acrylic paint.

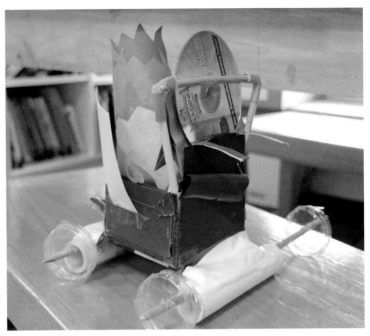

328 Melody's Wheelchair Design, Ella Levesque, Age 9, The Phoenix School,
Salem, MA; Materials: CDs, plastic lids, duct tape, wood pieces

329 Painted barrels, Arts in Nahant with Heather Goodwin, Ages 5–12;
Materials: metal trash cans and rustoleum paints

330 Pig Pen, Phoenix School Students, Salem, MA, Materials: plastic pigy banks
and paint

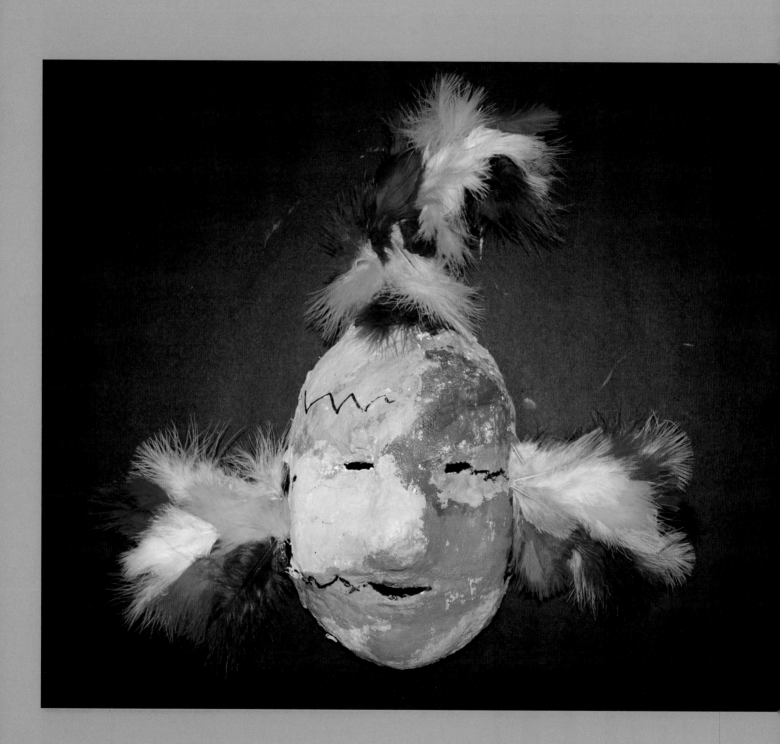

9. Sculpture and 3-D Art

Expressing an idea in three-dimensional form is no small feat but the range of materials to do so are unlimited. Classic papier-mâché and clay art are sculpture staples but this chapter also includes some exciting examples of how non-traditional approaches to sculpture can provide inventive ways to create in the round. Check out how a mound of tissue paper or salt crystals can become sculptures and the large-scale works like the Viking ship and dinosaurs!

331   Spooky Head, Young People's Group Children, Age 12, Cheshire, United Kingdom; Materials: Polystyrene ball, acrylic paints, miscellaneous lace/yarn/shredded plastic

332   Clothespin Creations, The Regal Find Artists, Ages 6–12; Materials: Clothespins, scrapbook paper, feathers, sequins, pipe cleaners, pom-poms

333   Wooden Camera, Asher and Arden, Ages 5 and 3; Materials: Scrap 2x4 wood chunks and variety of pre-made wooden shapes including colored checkers, wooden spools, buttons, circles, and hardboard scraps

334   Fantasty Forest. Stellan, Age 5; Materials: model magic, gold paper, paper straws, pipe cleaners and wire

335   Viking Ship, Lucius Armitage, Age 6; Materials: Two large cardboard boxes, paper plates for shields, a stick for a mast, paper for the sail, gaffer tape, rope, paint, and a giant imagination!

344   Bone Head, Otis Pippen, Age 9, with artist Siobhann Tarr, Bad Oldesloe, Germany; Materials: broken pieces of ceramics and glass, glue, grout and wooden base

345   Mosaic Sculpture, Loarn Ippen, Age 6 ,with artist Siobhann Tarr, Bad Oldesloe, Germany; Materials: Broken ceramics, mirror, colored glass, polystyrene cone, tile adhesive and grout

346   Dragon Dance Head, Alix Segil, Age 10; Materials: tissue and wrapping papers, recycled poster boards, commercial cardboard, foam, electrical tape, ribbons, rice paper, Velcro and pieces of wood

347   Ceramic Creature, Shota Brown, Age 10, Jordan Schnitzer Museum of Art, University of Oregon afterschool program; Materials: ceramics

348   Self-portrait, Jessica Age 10. Beverly, MA; Materials: wire, plaster bandages and paint

349   Panda, Gavin Minard, Age 10; Materials: Modeling clay and cardboard backing

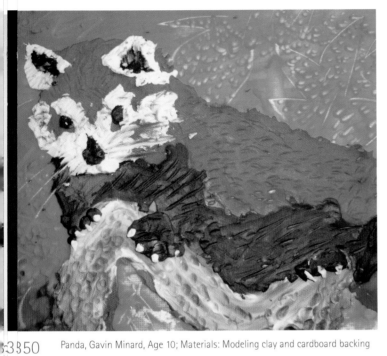

3350   Panda, Gavin Minard, Age 10; Materials: Modeling clay and cardboard backing

351   Insects, Lucas and Juliana Kaufman, Age 10; Materials: recycled paper pulp apple trays, pipe cleaners, plastic sheet, paper scraps, markers, and tempera paint

3352   Peg People, Asher and Arden, Ages 5 and 3; Materials: Wooden pegs and stars, acyrlic paint, felt, and fabric scraps

353   Stabile for Mom, Max, Age 9; Materials: Rock, acrylic paints, copper wire, cardstock, and pen

380   Wild Animal Carousel, Phoenix School
Students, Salem, MA Ages 5–13;
Materials: wood, wooden dowel, gold string,
acrylic paint

381   I Love Bananas, Susan Schwake's Art Lab
students; Materials: Pipe cleaners used to
create armature, rolled up magazine pages,
wooden beads, cardstock, markers and clay for
the base

382   Monster Container, Lindsay Hickey, in Nancy
Dapkiewicz's grade 8 art class at Stoneham
Middle School, Stoneham, MA;
Materials: fired clay and glazes

383   A Bird's Nest, Susan Schwake's Art Lab
students; Materials: Balloon to create form,
liquid glue to stiffen jute

384   Gnome Puppet, Susan Schwake's Art Lab
students; Materials: Low fire clay, clay tools,
and glazes

385   Pinch Pot Birds, Susan Schwake's Art Lab
students; Materials: White stoneware clay,
clay tools, glazes

386   Monster Container, Evan Taylor, in Nancy Dapkiewicz's grade 6 art class at Stoneham Middle School, Stoneham, MA; Materials: fired clay and glazes

387   Ceramic Spoonrest, Jane Buffo, in Nancy Dapkiewicz's grade 7 art class at Stoneham Middle School, Stoneham, MA; Materials: fired clay and glazes

388   Salt Crystal Sculpture, Sunshine Academy Toddler Program, Brookline, MA; Materials: water, salt and yarn.

389   Jumbo Mask, Susan Schwake's Art Lab students; Materials: cardboard box and tubes, miscellaneous found materials, papier mache glue, newspaper, acrylic paint and masking tape

396   Dragon Scene, Susan Schwake's Art Lab students; Materials: cut piece of wood for base, artificial plants, plastic dragon

397   A Bear's World, Susan Schwake's Art Lab students; Materials: cut piece of wood for base, artificial plants, bear, stemless wine glass for vitrine

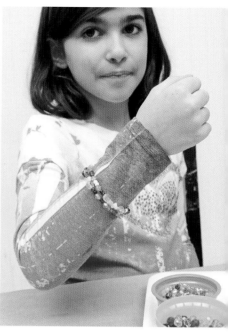

398   Bracelet, Susan Schwake's Art Lab students; Materials: memory wire and beads

399   Clay Puppets, Susan Schwake's Art Lab students; Materials: Low fire clay, clay tools, glazes

100   Bracelets, Family art program at the Peabody Essex Museum;
Materials: cut cardboard tubes, tin foil, embellishments

10. Sketches and Drawings

Starting as young as a year old, kids can use expressive strokes on paper to create art. Getting a crayon into the hands of young children as soon as possible sets the stage for the development of gross motor skills required to hold and then direct crayons and the like on paper to express themselves in a specific way as they grow. Kids' earliest drawings and sketches may not make much sense to the rest of us, but offering up the chance to be creative and expressive in our earliest years of life is an invaluable opportunity to start honing communication skills. Beyond crayons, markers, and pencils, this chapter includes yarn drawings, beautiful chalk pastel illustrations, and watercolor with ink study drawings.

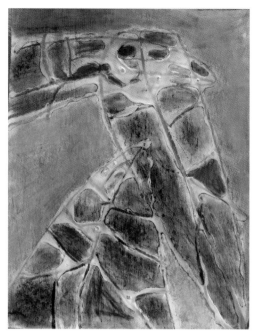

401   Fall Colors, Jack Owain Billowitz, Age 5;
Materials: Chalk and glue on paper

402   Fire Breathing Dragon, Krishna Divakarla, Age 9; Materials: Colored pencils on paper

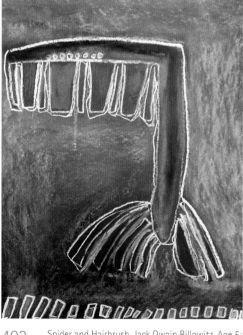

403   Spider and Hairbrush, Jack Owain Billowitz, Age 5;
Materials: Chalk on paper

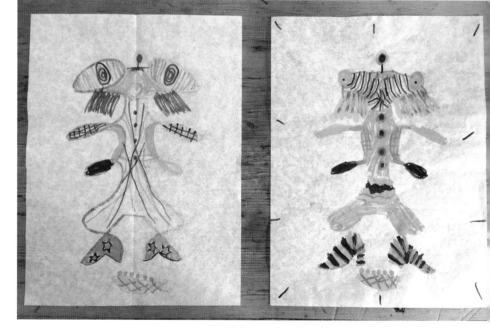

404   Mirror-Image Drawing, Alexandra Marie Hall, Age 9; Materials: Tracing paper and markers

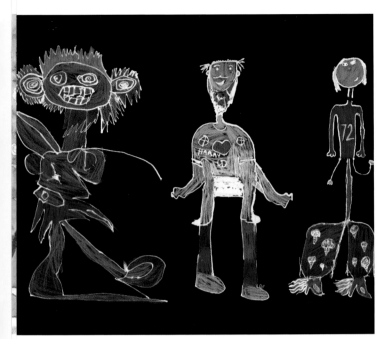

405   Exquisite Corps Drawing, Marcia Moore's K–5 art students at New Roads Elementary School, Los Angeles, CA, Age 5–10; Materials: black construction paper, whiteout pens, and colored pencils

406   No Rhyme or Reason Drawing, Tabitha French, Age 8; Materials: crayons and markers

407   Beach Drawing, Nick Blankenship, Age 7; Materials: markers on paper

408   Beeswax Crayon Drawing, Etta Spodick, Age 7 from Cape Ann Waldorf School, Beverly, MA; Materials: Stockmar beeswax crayon

423   Pop Art Self Portraits, Students from Our Lady
Seat of Wisdom Homeschool Cooperative
with Artists Brandie Pettus, Amherst, NH;
Materials: construction paper, glue and markers

424   Art Show, Mason, Age 4; Materials: crayon on paper

425   Pop Art Self Portraits, Students from Our Lady
Seat of Wisdom Homeschool Cooperative
with Artists Brandie Pettus, Amherst, NH;
Materials: construction paper, glue and markers

426   Chalk Art, Jonathan, Age 8; Materials: chalk on paper

27   Lion Dance, Stellan, Age 4; Materials: marker on paper

428   Playing Sports, Stellan, Age 4; Materials: maker on paper

29   The Beatles, Mason, Age 4; Materials: pen on paper

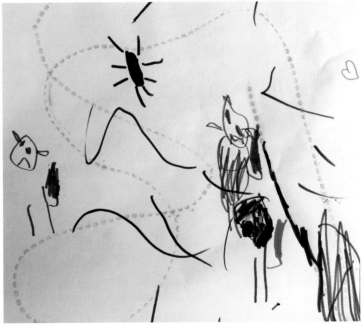

430   Yoda and Luke Skywalker, Mason, Age 4; Materials: markers on paper

431   Downtown Gloucester, Lila Hawks, Cape Ann
      YMCA summer camp, Gloucester, MA, Age 9;
      Materials: Pastels with marker

432   Knights, Sam Davis, Age 8; Materials: marker on paper

433   Rocketship, Sam Davis, Age 8;
      Materials: marker on paper

434   Fox Cave, Sam Davis, Age 8; Materials: marker on paper

35   Flowers, Lila Hawks, Age 8; Materials: crayons and sharpie on paper

436   Flowers, Lila Hawks, Age 7; Materials: watercolors and sharpie on paper

37   Camp, Lila Hawks, Age 8; Materials: watercolors and sharpie on paper

438   Mr. Moogle, Lila Hawks, Age 8; Materials: markers, permanent markers and crayons

439   Ink Drawing, Susan Schwake's Art Lab students; Materials: black ink, soft pastels and drawing paper

440   Scribble Drawing, Susan Schwake's Art Lab students; Materials: colored penci watercolors, and drawing paper

441   Scratch Art, Susan Schwake's Art Lab students; Materials: India ink on cardstock covered with crayon, small nail to scratch the design

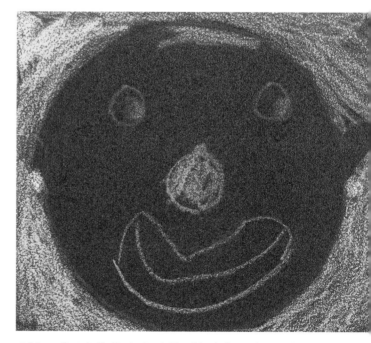

442   Portrait, Lila Hawks, Age 6; Materials: chalk pastels on sandpaper

443 Fauvist Portrait, Susan Schwake's Art Lab students; Materials: Charcoal, pencil, acrylic paint on canvas board

444 Landscape, Susan Schwake's Art Lab students; Materials: Charcoal, pencil, acrylic paint on canvas board

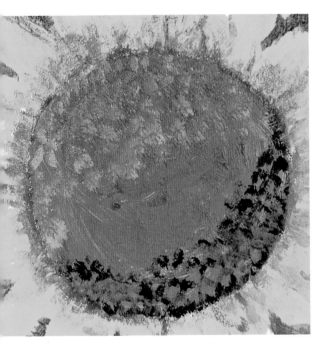

445 Sunflower, Susan Schwake's Art Lab students; Materials: Acrylic paint on primed wood

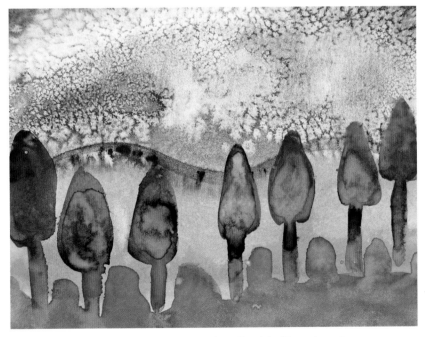

446 Landscape, Susan Schwake's Art Lab students; Materials: Watercolors, salt, sponge on watercolor paper

447   Pastel Drawing, Susan Schwake's Art Lab students; Materials: soft pastels on drawing paper

448   Teddy Bear Still Life, Susan Schwake's Art Lab students; Materials: Oil pastels on drawing paper

449   Self-Portrait, Isabella Riva, Age 4; Materials: pen and paint on paper

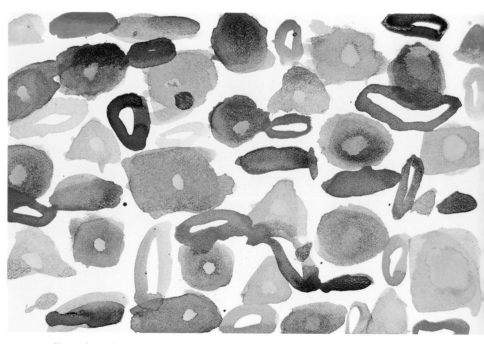

450   Shapes, Susan Schwake's Art Lab students; Materials: watercolors on watercolor paper

451 Snowmen Playing, Susan Schwake's Art Lab students; Materials: Oil pastels and watercolors on drawing paper

452 Ink Art, Susan Schwake's Art Lab students; Materials: Ink with dropper, oil pastels, straw and cardstock paper

453 Marble Drawing, Susan Schwake's Art Lab students; Materials: paint, marbles, cardstock, shoebox cover

454 Drawing on Fabric, Susan Schwake's Art Lab students; Materials: Pencil, oil pastels, cancas or heavy fabric, masking tape

464 Streets of Paris, Sam, Age 11, The Phoenix School, Salem, MA; Materials: watercolor on paper

465 Xochicalco, Mexico, Emma, Age 13, The Phoenix School, Salem, MA; Materials: watercolor on paper

-66   Arc de Triomphe, Sam, Age 11, The Phoenix School, Salem, MA; Materials: watercolor on paper

467 Taxco Square, Mexico, Emma, Age 13, The Phoenix School, Salem, MA; Materials: watercolor on paper

468 Fire and Ice, Joseph Luongo's 2nd grade Art Class, Malden, MA Public Schools; Materials: Construction paper, chalk pastels and paint

469   Georgia O'Keeffe Inspired Flower, Joseph Luongo's 7th grade Art Class, Malden, MA Public Schools; Materials: Oil pastels on paper

470   Candy, Joseph Luongo's 6th grade Art Class, Malden, MA Public Schools; Materials: oil pastelson paper

471   Keith Haring Style Drawing, Joseph Luongo's 4th grade Art Class, Malden, MA Public Schools; Materials: Colored cut paper and black permanent markers

472   Chuck Close Inspired Portrait, Joseph Luongo's 8th grade Art Class, Malden, MA Public Schools; Materials: Paper, colored pencil, airbrushed paints, printed images and cut paper

473   Hershey Bar, Joseph Luongo's 6th grade Art Class, Malden, MA Public Schools; Materials: oil pastels on paper

474   Chuck Close Inspired Portrait, Joseph Luongo's 8th grade Art Class, Malden, MA Public Schools; Materials: Colored pencil on paper

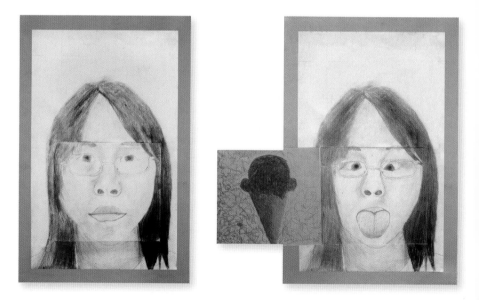

475   Two Part Portrait, Joseph Luongo's 8th grade Art Class, Malden, MA Public Schools; Materials: Pencil on paper

476   Chuck Close Inspired Portrait, Joseph Luongo's 8th grade Art Class, Malden, MA Public Schools; Materials: Colored pencil on paper

477   Portrait, Joseph Luongo's 8th grade Art Class, Malden, MA Public Schools; Materials: Printed photograph and pencil on paper

478   St John Snorkeling, Jeff, Age 13, The Phoenix School, Salem, MA; Materials: watercolor on paper

479   Keith Haring Style Drawing, Joseph Luongo's 4th grade Art Class, Malden, MA Public Schools; Materials: Colored cut paper and black permanent markers

480   My Thoughts Self Portrait, Joseph Luongo's 3rd grade Art Class, Malden, MA Public Schools; Materials: Colored paper, crayons and oil pastels

481   In the Manner OF Al Hirschfeld, Kala Plusquellic, in Nancy Dapkiewicz's grade 6 art class at Stoneham Middle School, Stoneham, MA; Materials: pen on paper

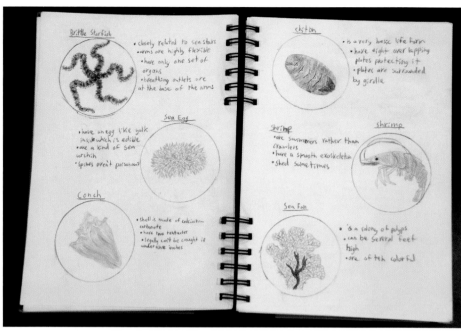

483   Flora and Fauna of St John's Waters, Jeff, Age, 13, The Phoenix School, Salem, MA;
Materials: watercolor on paper

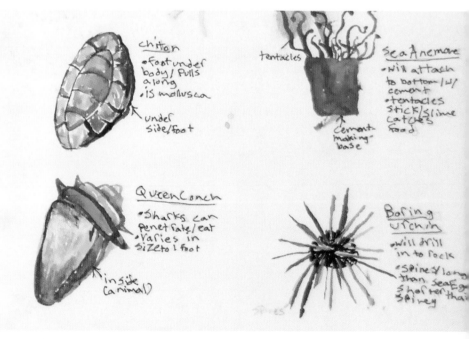

482   Animals of the World, The Phoenix School
students, Salem, MA Ages 5–12;
Materials: markers on paper

484   Creatures of the Caribbean, Antony, Age 10, The Phoenix School, Salem, MA;
Materials: watercolor on paper

485 Primary and Secondary Colors Drawing, created in Nancy Dapkiewicz's grade 6 art class at Stoneham Middle School, Stoneham, MA; Materials: cut paper and glue

486 Primary and Secondary Colors Drawing, created in Nancy Dapkiewicz's grade 6 art class at Stoneham Middle School, Stoneham, MA; Materials: cut paper and glue

487   Portrait, Susan Schwake's Art Lab students;
Materials: marker, acrylic paint on canvas board

488   Hundertwasser inspired Multi-media Collage, Amy Aker's 3rd grade art class, Chelmsford Public Schools, MA
Materials: permanent, metallic and watercolor markers, white paper, and colored metallic paper

489   Ink Art, Susan
Schwake's Art Lab
students; Materials:
India ink in a small
bottle, cotton swab
and paper

490   Happy Frog, Alicja Tokarska, Age 8; Materials: crayon on paper

11. Art and Technology

Being creative takes many forms and in the twenty-first century the range of creative tools available to artists is exploding. For example, tablet apps offer kids the chance to draw with their fingertips on a screen and then save and later print out their illustrations. This chapter shares some of the latest technologies that are used in creative form, including circuit stickers that light up with copper tape and watch batteries, digital photography and small creatures made with 3-D printing technologies.

491   The Letter P, 3D Font Design, Larchmont Charter
School, Fifth Grade, Los Angeles, CA, Age 10–11;
Materials: digital photograph

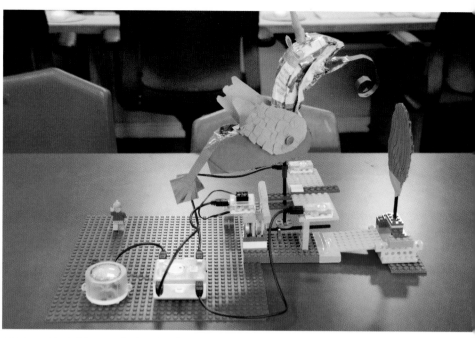

492   Mystical Creature, Student from The Phoenix School, Salem, MA; Materials: PicoCricket, building blocks,
cut paper, construction paper and markers

493   Digital Image Portraits, Joseph Luongo's 8th
grade art class, Malden, MA, public schools;
Materials: Digital portrait distorted with software,
cut paper and printed images

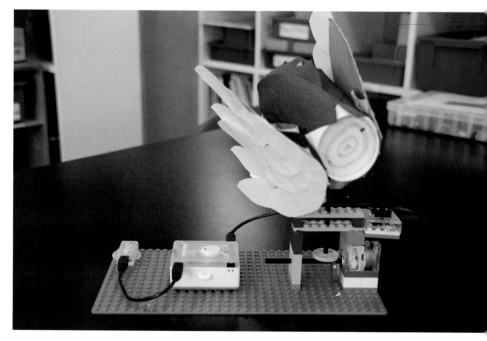

494   The Bird, Ella, Age 9 and Julia, Age 8, The Phoenix School, Salem, MA;
Materials: PicoCricket, coffee cups, construction paper and markers

95   The Thing, Mayan and Anthony, Age 12, The Phoenix School, Salem, MA;
Materials: PicoCricket, coffee cups and construction paper

496   A Face, ArtLink Youth Program for teens Peabody Essex Museum, Salem, MA; Materials: circuit stickers, paper, tracing paper, pen and pencil

497   Robot, ArtLink Youth Program, Peabody Essex Museum, Salem, MA; Materials: circuit stickers, paper, and colored pencils

498   Tunnel Vision, ArtLink Youth Program, Peabody Essex Museum, Salem, MA; Materials: circuit stickers, paper, and colored pencils

499   The Letter T, 3D Font Design, Larchmont Charter School, Fifth Grade, Los Angeles, CA, Age 10–11; Materials: digital photograph

The Letter A, 3D Font Design, Larchmont Charter School, Fifth Grade, Los Angeles, CA, Age 10–11;
Materials: digital photograph

CONTRIBUTOR DIRECTORY

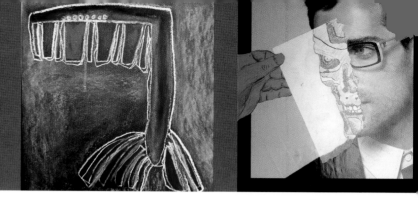

ACKNOWLEDGMENTS

THANK YOU to each and every one of the contributors to this publication: parents, educators, and colleagues. Your efforts to teach, support and celebrate each of the young artists in this book are inspiring. And to all of the artists—don't ever stop creating!

ABOUT THE AUTHOR

GAVIN ANDREWS is an art educator and artist based in Boston, Massachusetts. She is dedicated to the role art and creativity can play in everyone's life and is passionate about empowering kids and adults alike with the tools of creative self-expression.

Gavin has a range of academic and professional experiences that don't follow a straight line but cumulatively shape her approach to the arts. Currently she works at the Peabody Essex Museum, in Salem, Massachusetts, where she collaborates with artists, educators, community leaders, students and youth, so the museum can respond as a center for creativity, learning, and social engagement.

Her previous work has included research on material cultural in the late Bronze Age in Israel, she has studied and documented the impact of large-scale public art in communities and chaired an arts commission tasked with grant ing funds to community artists. She has a BA in art & art history from the University of Texas at Austin, an MS in arts administration from Boston University, and professional training in program evaluation. She speaks regularly as a guest lecturer at universities and presents nationally on innovative approaches to engagement in the arts through museums.

She lives with her husband, Lance, and their two young children, Stellan and Elsa, who also happen to be her favorite artists.